WILTSHIRE

A COUNTY GUIDE

Including Bath and Avon

Stonehenge

Wiltshire: a County Guide
Including Bath and Avon

Copyright © 2012 Cv Publications
All rights reserved

The right has been asserted by N.P.James
to be identified as the author of this work under
the Copyright, Designs and Patents Act of 1988

ISBN 978-1-908419-12-5

Barnaby's Relocation Guides ISSN: 1466-6634

British Library Cataloguing in Publication Data.
A Catalogue record of this book is available from the British Library.

Set in 10pt Book Antiqua. Photographs and page design
by Cv/Visual Arts Research. Copyright reserved.

This is a digital format publication
Printed and bound by Blissett: Design.Print.Media
www.blissettdigital.co.uk

Readers are advised to obtain two customers' references
before proceeding with a particular service listed in
Wiltshire: a County Guide
The Editors and Publisher do not accept responsibility for any loss or
damage to home or business incurred from a reader's use of a listed service

Editorial address

Cv Publications
10 Barley Mow Passage
Chiswick, London W4 4PH
www.tracksdirectory.ision.co.uk

Introduction

The sixth in Cv's series of English County Guides explores Wiltshire. The dramatic sweep of a spare landscape of the Pewsey Vale introduces the historic town of Marlborough. It follows routes towards the West; to Bath and Avon; taking in settlements of Chippenham, Calne, Melksham, , Devizes, Malmesbury and Bradford on Avon.

The Author at the Royal Crescent Hotel, Bath, February 2012

Wiltshire is beautiful and mysterious, spanned by ancient lay lines and runic landmarks such as Stonehenge, The White Horse and the Avebury Ring. This is an original account of eye-witness experience; fascinating for visitors and informative for those seeking a new place to live.

First researched from 1999-2001 and resumed in 2011-12, Cv's series of English County Guides provides descriptions of market towns and villages, for casual visitors and those interested in moving to a different area.

The guides contain eye-witness records of natural character, of the villages: the properties, amenities, communication, travel and business links. Available titles include: Oxfordshire, Gloucestershire, Buckinghamshire, Cornwall, Norfolk and Wiltshire; Cumbria is in preparation for autumn 2012.

Each guide records between one and two hundred villages and county towns. There are route maps, colour photographs, and a directory of local services.

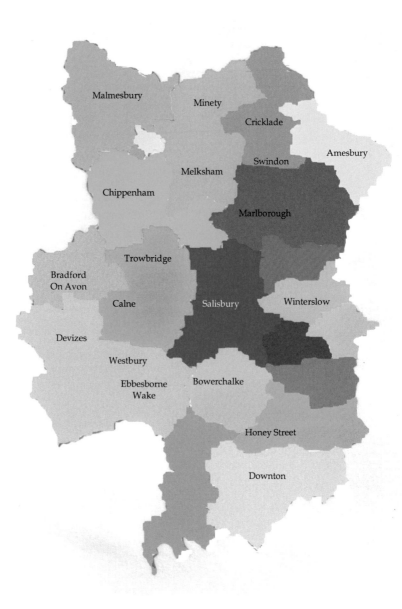

WILTSHIRE

Marlborough Wiltshire

Lopcombe Corner

The three settlements of West Winterslow, Middle Winterslow and East Winterslow were collectively named in the Domesday Book in 1086 as Wintreslei, meaning "Winter's mound or burial place". Lying approximately six miles east of Salisbury, along a 500 foot high ridge, the three settlements were composed of separate manors which would develop their own manorial histories
history.wiltshire.gov.uk/community/

*Art Club at Fordingbridge*Twelve miles from West Winterslow there are monthly demonstrations in Avonway on the 1st Sunday of the month.
fordingbridgeart@forestmoods.co.uk

First journey 7th July 2011
Just turned off the A30 at Lopcombe Corner to reach the Winterslows, villages right on the Hampshire/ Wiltshire border. Driving into very pretty countryside, idyllic, a gentle span of fields. This seems to be a comfortable residential situation. Proceeding towards Middle Winterslow to visit Roche Court, the sculpture garden and collection of Madeleine Ponsonby, ex New Art Centre.

Comfortably appointed bungalows sitting behind the yew hedges, a fresh day with a gentle breeze coming off the hills. Andover and Stockbridge to the left, West Winterslow is ahead.

West Winterslow

West Winterslow

Approached through a shaded avenue of trees; building work going on here on a white cottage. High banked walls protecting residences with their substantial front lawns. The local bus passes, a number 89. Winterslow straggles over a wide area, penetrated by a narrow single track road. The new build on the outskirts is attractive with a note of weather board on its frontage.

  N.J. Rowe Investment and Development is here. *The Shooting Box*, a long cream painted house; Land Rovers parked in front. Another little settlement: a barn, a post box stuck on a post. Big old farm barn in an apple orchard. Blackmore Copse and East Grimstead are in the vicinity.

Winterslow Primary
A church school at the heart of Winterslow village which is only eight miles from the city of Salisbury. Christian values lie at the heart of the school life, Approximately one hundred and seventy pupils on roll

Winterslow CE Primary School, Winterslow, Salisbury, SP5 1RD T: 01980 862446

A Spring Show is held at Winterslow Village Hall in March; Winterslow Parish Church Fete is held in July. www.winterslow.org.uk/

Visit Salisbury and South Wiltshire Museum
The Kings House,
65 The Close, SP1 2EN
01722 332151

The Rifles (Berkshire and Wiltshire) Museum
The Wardrobe, 58 The Close, Salisbury, Wiltshire, SP1 2EX, Tel: +44 (0)1722 419419

East Grimstead

Reading Room
The new building was opened in 1995 and is available to hire for Meetings, Private Parties, Dances, Wedding Receptions, Concerts & Plays The Reading Room has excellent facilities for the disabled. There is an annual Hot Cross Bun Morning held at the hall. Staging is available for performances. www.southwilts.com/site/East-Grimstead-Reading-Room/

Property values
Detached freehold properties at East Grimstead valued at £771,633 and £1,408,101 (March 2012) Zoopla.co.uk

Dean Hill Park contains over two hundred plant species including ten varieties of orchid, monitored by an active conservation group. deanhillpark.org.uk

East Grimstead

A big logging unit here, interesting place. Driving through a forest, Farley and Pitton to the right. A sign for *'Power Training in the Forest'*, but we're not quite in the military area here. A mix of styles, a little patch of common land bordered by period properties. A tall cone roofed 19th century house, then a small gothic regency with those decorative hooped windows. A comfortable, well maintained landscape. Under a low bridge with a slosh of rain water, into open wheatfields, not quite ready for harvest, past scraps of sheds and disused farm implements.

Sheep grazing at Yew Tree Farm, Bowerchalke

West Dean

East Brothers Saw Mill and Timber Yard is based at West Dean along with Dean Hill Park Light Industrial Estate. A detailed design of West Dean Community and activities is available at www.southwilts.com/site/West-Dean-PC/

Property Values

Five bed.detached modern freehold in Laverstock £305K (Fox & Sons)

Three bed detached bungalow £234,950 (Connells, Salisbury)

Work out at

Five Rivers Leisure Centre Hulse Rd Salisbury Wiltshire SP1 3NR www.wiltshire.gov.uk/leisureandrecreation/leisureandsportscentres/lscsalisburyfiverivers

West Dean

Towards the Winterslows, heavily overhung trees; an attractive old thatched cottage. A level crossing and then a common. West Dean Saw Mill is the centre of activity, you hear the band saws buzzing away.

Passing the Hill Top Diner on the way to Salisbury, overlooking a broad sweep of Wiltshire downland. Figsbury Ring is a local landmark. Salisbury, Laverstock, Ford on the A30. The Silver Plough for hospitality. A side road leads away on Old Malthouse Lane. Park and Ride for the cty centre, five miles away, is here. The spire of Salisbury Cathedral in the centre of the horizon. The Duck Inn is one mile away.

Laverstock . Salisbury .

Laverstock and Salisbury

A clutch of red brick 2/3 bed homes. Bishop's Mead, a residential close. It has a school, a modern glass building: St Edmunds Girls School and Sports College. Lots of new build and occasionally a gabled antique 17th century. More new build in Mayfair Close—council house modern. Then a sign *'Welcome to Salisbury, twinned with St.*Etienne'. The Laverstock Road leads uphill bordered by council houses. The Godolphin School is here, the built up and the road narrows down Milford Hill past red brick Victorian terraces into Salisbury. Ahead is the city centre, in a higgledy piggledy layout, quaint styles and mixed periods of building. Coming down by Guilder Street and Culver

Local Schools

St Andrew's CofE VA Primary School
Church Road, Laverstock, Wiltshire, SP1 1QX
Telephone: 01722 503590 Fax: 01722 503590
Age Range: 4-11

St Edmund's CofE Girls' School
Church Road, Laverstock, Wiltshire, SP1 1RD
Telephone: 01722 328565
Email: officmail@stedmunds.rmplc.co.uk
Website: www.st-edmundsgirls.wilts.sch.uk
Age Range: 11-16

Wyvern College
Church Road, Laverstock, Wiltshire, SP1 1RE
Telephone: 01722 500700 Fax: 01722 500900
Age Range: 11-16
www.alltheschools.com/wiltshire/laverstock

Salisbury

Cathedral Services
Tuesday 13th March 2012
07:30 - Morning Worship with Holy Communion
12:15 - Holy Communion, CW Order 1, Chapel of St Edmund and St Thomas
17:30 - Choral Evensong
Wednesday 14th March 2012
07:30 - Morning Worship with Holy Communion
09:15 - Staff Prayers
12:15 - Informal Concert
17:30 - Choral Evensong
19:30 - The Bible in the Cathedral

Salisbury City Council
The Guildhall Market Place
Salisbury Wiltshire SP1 1JH
Tel: 01722 342860

Local News
Follow local news and events in the Salisbury Journal
www.salisburyjournal.co.uk/

Street, with its Regency façade.

Wiltshire Museum Service staged an excellent survey of John Constable. Staying with his friend and supporter Dr John Fisher, the artist worked here at intervals, through to 1831. Loaned by the V&A, the Tate, the Ashmolean: most interesting, amongst famous studies are some little drawings; a terrific watercolour made at night of a house by a bridge, with the nerve edged tension that distinguishes his work. Constable, less fantastical, but I feel rings more true than JMW Turner, who was such a wizard and alchemist.

Then to the outskirts, proceeding uphill near Mayrick Avenue; largely Victorian terraces. leading to Bouverie Avenue and back down Bouverie

Aspect of Salisbury Cathedral

Window shopping in Marlborough

Coffe Break at Trowbisdge

Longboats moored at the Barge Inn in the Pewsey Valley

Market Day, Devizes

Wilton

Winning Streak
Regular events and competi-
tive race meetings at Salisbury Race Course
Bar, enclosure, grandstand,
disabled facilities Tickets
available online
www.salisburyracecourse.co.uk/
Salisbury Racecourse,
Netherhampton, Salisbury,
Wiltshire SP2 8PN

Theatregoer
Salisbury Playhouse
Malthouse Lane,
Salisbury, Wiltshire SP2 7RA
01722 320 333
www.salisburyplayhouse.com/

Arts Centre
Salisbury Arts Centre is
housed in the deconsecrated
church building on Bedwin
Street and is easy to get to by
car, bus, train and foot. Look
out for our brightly coloured
flags.
Salisbury Arts Centre, Bedwin
Street, Salisbury, SP1 3UT
Tel: 01722 321744
www.salisburyartscentre.co.uk/

Avenue into Salisbury to find the A36 and the ring road to Marlborough on the A338.

Wilton

Pretty, crowded, confused. Once a beautiful Regency settlement; now sadly ruined - its village green sliced in two by a main road, with heavy continuous traffic pumping through, to and from Salisbury, quite obliterating the attractive period residences that border the common. Here are the ceremonial gates to Wilton House, the historic estate and very popular visitor destination. Across the road you can enjoy hospitality at The Pembroke Arms.

Sign to Fosbury

The road to Alvediston

The Vale of Alvediston

Bowerchalke

Footpath, Calne

Great Wishford

Great Wishford C.E. (V.A.)
Primary School
West Street Great Wishford
Salisbury Wiltshire SP2 0PQ
Tel: 01722 790433
admin@greatwishford.wilts.
sch.uk

History, Directory, What's On
at Great Wishford
www.greatwishford.co.uk

Hanging Langford Cam
is the remains of an Iron
Age / Romano British settlement linked to an enclosure
known as Church-End Ring.

Great Wishford

The lane to Great Wishford, just broader than a single track, winding amidst silvery, heavy foliaged trees. Fresher countryside than the north side of the county. A pedestrian footpath leads through the fields to an obscure settlement. Great Wishford has very pretty thatched cottages down below the road; in King's Mead there are modernish properties. Detached bungalows spread along to West Street and The Royal Oak. A little cemetery on the outskirts. Little Langford and Hanging Langford are neighbours. Narrow roads but very pretty, overhung with weeping willows and beside runs a stream. Sheep and cattle grazing, a quiet place - idyllic. Fields planted up with barley and kale.

Little Langford

The landscape includes a house in trees, enclosed in this tranquil setting. Past a big barn adjoining a working farm. Cattle penned - their droppings all along the road. The hills look like perfect artificial mounds, Saxon funeral barrows?

At Wiltshire Museums I encountered a stone sarcophagus dug up from an ancient barrow. It contained the body of a woman with fur lined slippers made of deerskin, cradling a child. She wore a jet amulet. Remains from thousands of years ago.

Little Langford

A spare settlement, just a single track lane, sitting in an up and down landscape of paddocks and individual period properties. Little Langford Farmhouse, a nice place to stay

Wilton House and Old Riding School 5th May-2nd September Sun-Thur 11.30am-4.30pm Last Adm 3.45pm Grounds 5th May-16th September 11am-5pm Last adm 4.30pm
House and Grounds
Adult £14 / Concession £11.25/Child (5-15) £7.50 Family ticket (2 adults and 2 children 5-15 incl) £34.00

Wilton Salisbury SP2 0BJ
Tel: 01722 746700

Great Wishford C.E. (V.A.) Primary School
West Street Great Wishford Salisbury Wiltshire SP2 0PQ
Tel: 01722 790433:
admin@greatwishford.wilts.sch.uk

History, Directory, What's On at Great Wishford
www.greatwishford.co.uk/

Hanging Langford

B&B
Little Langford Farm House
Little Langford alisbury
Wiltshire P3 4NP
Telephone   01722 790205
www.littlelangford.co.uk/
contact.htm

Little Langford Down
Remote chalk downland site to
the west of Salisbury.
www.wiltshire-web.co.uk/
oldwildlife/

Hanging Langford Camp is the
remains of an Iron Age /
Romano British settlement
linked to an enclosure known
as Church-End Ring.

Property for Sale
Hanging Langford, 2 bed, 1
recept. Character property
£350K. *(Chesterton/Humberts)*

Up the hill, washing out on the line flapping in the fresh breeze. This is the beginning of the Wylie Valley, with strings of villages going to the West. Lines of poplars give a French feel to the view.

Hanging Langford

A dramatic name, that speaks of a dark history. Yew trees shielding substantial stone built houses. No store sighted. A church; roses growing up a thatched cottage, another has a pattern of chequerboard white and grey flint. Quite a long high street. A property sold by Clifford and Drew. Symonds and Sampson are holding a sale by auction in the village hall. Hollyhocks laced into the banks of a cottage, buttercups and cow parsley in the hedgrows.

Wylye

Wylye

At the head of the Wylye Valley in an open span landscape, modest and pretty. Next to the Langfords and not too far from the A303. It benefits from rich farmland. A string of 1950s houses, cars pulled in off road. Thatched Jacobean cottages. Wylye is quite big, a post office (closed) and The Bell Inn. Various choice properties with their own courtyards, streams, flowering arbours. A choice Georgian house is sighted in the trees.

Second Journey,

Friday 18th November 2011

Turned off the A346 from Swindon to Marlborough, and aiming to explore some of the villages in the Wylye Valley. Ogbourne St.Andrew ahead, on a silvery day.

Wylye Valley Vineyard is at Crockerton, about 600 yards along the A350 road to Poole, just south of the main A36 Bath-Salisbury road

Mill Farm House
Hill Deverill Wiltshire
www.ukvines.co.uk/vineyards/wylye

After School Club

Wylye Coyotes Afterschool Club has a den in the grounds of Wylye Valley School, available for children, as and when they wish.
www.wylyecoyotes.com/index.htm

Wylye Valley Clay Shooting Ground is located at Deptford Field Barn, Wylye, Wiltshire BA12 0QL
www.wylye-shooting.co.uk/

Postern Hill

Camping in the Forest holiday at Postern Hill.
The Caravan Park and Camp-site located in the Savernake Forest, which is privately owned and run by The Forestry Commission.
Postern Hill Marlborough Wiltshire SN8 4ND T: 01672 515195
www.campingintheforest.co.uk/our_sites

The shape of Wiltshire is rather eccentric. The north side has Marlborough and Tidworth with its military base, and large memorial cemeteries. Then there's the vast Salisbury Plain, used for training and exercises. Strings of old settlements below the plain, and a secondary level on the way towards Bath, with the historic towns of Chippenham, Trowbridge, Melksham, Calne and Devizes.

Wltshire resembles an ornate fretted cake. In this season the fields are laid to rest; sheared, ploughed, levelled off.

Postern Hill
Set in wooded parkland outside Marlborough. The road leads from Wilton to Teffont Magna.

Collingbourne

Coming through Cadley on the A436, with an avenue of autumn trees. Little gothic and thatched cottages here, set in their spacious gardens. An attractive nook. You have the Royal Oak B&B; Brimslade and Burbage are a neighbours. A farm barn for sale by Carter Jonas, low lying, off the road. There's the Three Horseshoes Inn for hospitality.

Salisbury, Collingbourne and Kingston are twenty miles ahead. A rather nondescript landscape of pylons and little wooden cabins, a green one sighted providing a car repair service. All the same, there's a dramatic effect to the surrounding hills, making long slug shapes, dark on the horizon. The Barleycorn Inn serves food here as one enters

The Parish Council awards grants or makes donations to local clubs and organisations in order to support causes which it considers beneficial to the Parish, to promote local activity, and to support clubs and organisations in applying for grants elsewhere. www.collingbourne-ducis.com/

Materials used in the construction of the older buildings consist of mainly local brick, often speckled red, and rubble and flints was used to build walls. These walls were often covered in lime wash and some modern developments were required, as a planning requirement to white paint their walls to harmonise with the older properties nearby. www.collingbourne-ducis.com/

Collingbourne Ducis

Leckford Cricket Club
Invites potential players to get
involved in the wide range of
activities
Browse leckfordcc.play-
cricket.com/ for membership
details

Collingbourne Kingston on the A346, on a low lit winter's day.

A random cluster of modest properties on the main Salisbury Road. The centre has 15th century timber and plaster buildings.

A garage shop and a line of detached modern houses. It has a village hall. Collingbourne Ducis is a neighbour. Cadley Gardens Trading Estate is here and the Shears Inn.

Collingbourne Ducis

An attractive solid settlement on the A346 to Salisbury. It has lots of thatched properties. Adam Nash, master tradesman, operates here. The village is widespread, bungalows up the hill and council stock on the outskirts to the fields.

Leckford . Cholderton . =

Leckford

On the way to Salisbury on the A338, Leckworth is invisible,nothing sighted. A sign points to Trenchard Lines, Ludyards Hall is nearby, Tidworth and its military encampment, is one mile away. Crossing into Hampshire at Shipton Bellinger and then back into Wiltshire.

Cholderton

Along the A338. With its pretty avenue of trees giving onto the fields, with horses grazing. Rather an exclusive area, with lanes leading to major residences shielded by low walls. A rare breeds farm is here. Warm gold tints of the late autumn. Newton Tony off to the left; Allington is ahead. The Mallet Arms Restaurant provides hospitality.

Cholderton Rare Breeds Farm Park
Amesbury Road, Cholderton, Salisbury, Wilts SP4 0EW
Tel/Fax: 01980 629438
Open season: 15 March-
3 November
Opening times: 10.00 am -
6.00 pm
(last admission 4.45 pm)
Admission: Adult £5.50;
Child £3.50; Senior Citizen/
Disabled £4.50; Family £13.00

.Crown Inn
The Crown Inn sits right at the heart of the village of Cholderton on the A338 ten miles north of Salisbury on the border of Wiltshire and Hampshire in the picturesque Bourne Valley
www.crowncholderton.com/

Allington . Boscombe .

The Old Inn, Tidworth Road,
Allington, Salisbury,
Wiltshire, SP4 0BN
01980 619045

The place-name, Boscombe,
which first appears in the
Domesday Book of 1086 as
Boscumbe, very likely means
'valley overgrown with spiky
plants (Gorse?)', from the Old
English **bors + cumb.*
www.roman-britain.org/places/
boscombe.

Boscombe Village Gardens
Boscombe, Wiltshire, SP4
0AB
*Opening dates and times:*Sun
19, Mon 20 Feb (11-4); Sun 8,
Mon 9 Apr, Sun 6, Mon 7
May (2-5).
Admission:Combined adm
£4.50, chd free
www.ngs.org.uk/gardens/

Allington

On the A338, Salisbury about seven miles away. A rather interesting new architectural development. A tower with a glass cupola. Dine at the Old In Restaurant.

Boscombe

Flint faced farm, a big barn. Tucked away to the side is Old Boscombe, giving out on to a hillside. The Earl of Normanton. Buildings pitched uip on the side of the road, one resembling a Methodist chapel. Idmiston is a neighbour, Porton Down is ahead.

Winterbourne Gunner

Situated on the A346, a most impressive weatherboarded barn with a great thatched roof. Typical of this area, the soft conical thatch-capped over plaster wattle and timber frame.

Winterbourne Dauntsey

Winterbourne Dauntsey

Even its Mace Store and Post Office is thatched, charming. It has a school, an Inn. One of the bigger Winterbournes, leads to Winterbourne Earls. Red brick 1950s in Tanners Close. Hurdcott down a narrow lane is a neighbour. In sight of the spire of Salisbury Cathedral. Wonderful light, real Constable country. Laverstock and Stockbridge are nearby. The Duck inn at Laverstock for refreshment. Brewers Fayre provides accommodation in the vicinity. Then the industrial units and car dealerships introduce Salisbury city centre.

Turned off the main road, the A30 to Shaftesbury, to Alvediston deep in the heart of Wiltshire.

Salisbury Country Market
Charter Market Market Square
Salisbury SP1 1JH
Opening: Saturday, 7.30 am - 2.30 pm

www.bigbarn.co.uk/marketplace/vendors/salisbury

Alvediston

The Crown Inn, Alvediston,
Salisbury, SP5 5JY
The Crown has a formal
dining room, which can can be
booked for large parties
and functions including
birthday parties, family events
or as a meeting place for businesses and clubs. It can also
be booked for shoot meals
from October until February
Telephone: 01722 - 780335

St Mary, Alvediston
A 17th century church restored
in 1886, is home to the grave of
Anthony Eden, Earl of Avon
(1897-1977),
One bell of three, dated 1663,
is still in use.

First sighted in this beautiful land-scape, is South Farm, caring for sheep fields, with the downs rising up overseeing this special area. A single track lane rising uphill. At the top great views of the spreading countryside, completely peaceful.

No sight of a river here, dry land, but very beautiful. A fine horse in its winter coat. The land rises and banks in levels, so there's one range of hills before another. Descending into Alvediston past great copper-leafed hedges that front a substantial stone built and thatched roofed property, then an 18th century bank of cottages, curiously supported on a walled rampart. Very picturesque.

Ebbesborne Wake

Ebbesborne Wake

Avoiding the Somerset border I turn left back to Salisbury. An old chapel boarded up, a pale blue weathered door, disused and stuck out alone in the fields. A cast iron decorative sign announces *Trunyons*, a small white cottage in its own grounds. Ebbesborne Wake is found here, tucked in the downs. A white fence borders the road, intersected at intervals by small footbridges, that lead to the old dwellings.

Duck Street is impenetrable for my estate car, so proceed along May Lane instead. The road descends steeply into the village, the Hollow leads away in the trees. McKillop Gregory has an attractive long white cottage for sale here.

Fragmentary records from Saxon times (circa 826 AD) indicate that the whole Chalke Valley area was thriving, and the village was called Ebles-burna. It is surmised that the land adjacent to the River Bourne was once owned by a man called Ebbel.[3] Note that the word bourne is derived from the Old English "brunna". *Source Wikipedia* Ebbesbourn Wake

Property for Sale
5 Beds, 3 Baths, House, Garden, Terrace, Garage, Reception £995K
2 Beds, 1 Bath, House, Garden, Fireplace, Parking, Cottage, Central Heating £330K
(nestoria.co.uk)

Accommodation
Lancers House*** Sutton Mandeville, Salisbury, SP3 5NL
3.84 kilometers from Ebbesbourne Wake. Room prices starting from £60

Avebury

Martin's Workshop, Fifield Bavant.

Public Garden, Emery Walk, Chippenham

Town Centre, Chippenham

Bowerchalke . Fifield Bavant .

Bowerchalke B&B
Greenbank Bed & Break-
fast
Church Street Bowerchalke-
Salisbury SP5 5BE
Telephone   01722 780350

Yoga Classes
in Bowerchalke Village Hall
on Tuesday mornings 9.30 -
11 am.
All ages and abilities are very
welcome
Bowerchalke Village Hall
Church Street, Bowerchalke,
Salisbury, Wiltshire, SP5
5BE
www.chalkevalley.org.uk

St.Martin's Church
the smallest church in Wiltshire and the second smallest
in England still in regular use
for worship.
www.chalkevalley.org.uk/
fifield-bavant/

The Horseshoe Inn for a drink and a snack. In Pound Street and some new build developments, in tune with traditional styles: stone built. A very pretty blue cottage is hidden in the trees, tucked safely in the hills.

Bowerchalke and Fifield Bavant
Underneath Salisbury, in a valley that runs along to Shaftesbury. Gentle fields with low banked hills, an old church perched on the top. Fifield has the Manor Farm and a cluster of old properties. Sheep grazing everywhere, in this deep countryside. Then Broad-chalke, a few low lying bungalows overlooking the vale. An impressive thatched property, broadly disposed. A dry gully and a small duck pond. It straggles along, proving to be quite a substantial settlement.

Bishopstone

The Queen's Head Inn,a church, and a bus stop. Overhanging willows draw from a stream running beside the road. It has a school and a village sports centre. Rural, but in easy reach of Salisbury city centre. Stoke Farm manages the land. Stoke Farthing is a neighbour.

Bishopstone

On a B road towards Salisbury. Here is Flamstone Farm and a mixture of modern properties off the road. It has the White Hart Inn and a village hall. A novel dwellingwith a load of whirligigs spinning in front of it. A metal silhouette identifies Meadow Rise cottage. Bishopstone Parish Church to the right and pretty pink washed Regency cottages. And along this way we

Longleat Safari Park
The Safari Park, Adventure Park, Longleat House and all attractions open from Saturday 11th February.
Open Daily: Saturday 11th Feb to Sunday 19th Feb
Open Saturday & Sundays: Saturday 25th Feb to Sunday 18th March
Open Daily: Saturday 24th March to Sunday 4th Nov
Tel: 01985 844400
www.longleat.co.uk/plan-your-visit/

Six Hamlets
The village of Bishopstone can date its history back to the 12th century when it is first recorded as the parish of Bissopeston in 1166. The church of St John the Baptist was built at about this time. Bishopstone actually consists of sixHamlets: Croucheston, Faulston, Netton, Flamstone, Throope and Bishopstone.
http://www.bishopstone-salisbury.co.uk/

Coombe Bissett

Dramatic Society

Coombe Bissett and Homington Drama Club was formed in 1973 just after the Coombe Bissett and Homington Village Hall was first built in 1972. The club generally puts on a pantomime in the village hall during the first week of December and a play in May
www.coombebissett.com

Local School

Coombe Bissett
CE VA Primary School
Shutts Lane Coombe Bissett
SP5 4LU T: 01722 19390

Property for Sale

Period two/potential three bedroom detached property, formerly the old school house with the original school bell, in the heart of the village
£360K *(Whites)*

find Stratford Tony. Wilton is nearby. Stratford Tony has a farm, while the village spreads away, with a mixture of modest Victorian and Georgian properties. Not large, but set in an idyllic downland landscape. Busy traffic coming through, it's a main link to Shaftesbury.

Coombe Bissett

Near Salisbury, at the head of the valley, with detached substantial houses, modernish, with their own gravelled forecourts, looking onto level water meadows. In reach of the A303. Bake Fruit Farm is here, by the copper beech avenue leading towards Salisbury. Homington is a neighbour.

Chippenham

23rd November

Walking down Timber Street, from the Emery Gate car park at the back end of Chippenham, I come upon the old Bear Hotel, an impressive 17th century red brick building fronting the the main thoroughfare.

It's a quiet midweek day in the market town. The predominantly Queen Anne buildings are made with blocks of pale grey Bath stone.

The sign points to the Emery Gate and the Wiltshire history centre, post office and tourist information. A war memorial is sheltered by a roofed colonnaded structure that frames an introduction to the shopping precinct, the Merry Gate Shopping Centre, an impressive new mall, with its blue framed conical

Stay at
The Angel Hotel,
Market Place,
Chippenham, Wiltshire SN15
3HD, UK Tel: 01249 652 615

Chippenham Town Council
The Town Hall High Street
Chippenham Wiltshire
SN15 3ER
T: 01249 446699

Chippenham Events
September witnesses the Chippenham Open Challenge Fishing Match on the River Avon, together with the Beer Festival. October sees a Classic Car Rally and celebrates 50's rock with the annual Eddie Cochran Festival.
www.cotswolds.info/places/chippenham

Chippenham Sports Club
Bristol Road, Chippenham
SN15 1NG
01249 652 867

Chippenham

Reel Chippenham
Cinema, Marshfield Road,
Chippenham
01509 221 155

Chippenham Town FC
Plays in the Southern League
Premier Division and is based
at
Hardenhuish Park
Bristol Road Chippenham
Wiltshire SN14 6LR
Tel: 01249 650400

Home news
Shopping, trade services are
listed on Chippenham People
www.chippenhampeople.co.u
k/home

The Rotary Club of Chippenham
The Rotary Hall
16 Station Hill Chippenham
SN15 1EG
enquir-
ies@chippenhamrotary.org.
www.chippenhamrotary.org/

roof. The arcade includes Timsons Locksmiths, a Fragrance Store, Sports Direct, Peacocks Clothing, Holland & Barratt Health Foods next to the YMCA; it's a big arcade. Alternatively you can explore the Borough Parade, and more stores. Waitrose, The Body Shop, Entertainment Exchange and Robert Dyas. For a more peaceful environ go to the riverside, where you can lunch at the Bridge House, a Wetherspoons pub listed in the Good Beer Guide 2012.

Here are some good looking town houses with decorative blue steps to the first floor entrance – *The River Parade*. From here you sight the Victorian aqueduct, a tall train bridge. Pleasant parkland beside the water, busy with crowds of

Pewsham

demanding swans and seagulls. Drop into the Chippenham History Museum, an intriguing section on the town police. In 1841 the uniform was white trousers, a dark blue tailcoat with silver buttons, and a broad top hat with a badge on it, which morphed into the more familiar conical policeman's helmet.

On to Calne and Devizes on the A4, past the magistrates court on the outskirts of Chippenham. Some modern developments here giving onto the pleasant aspects of gentle fields, then very quickly into farm land. Abbey Fields School is here, on the London Road

Pewsham, on the A4 going towards Calne. Just a tiny settlement, but it has got the Wiltshire and Berkshire

The Lysley Arms Main Road, Pewsham, Chippenham SN15 3RU. (01249) 652864

For Sale
Modern 4 bedroom detached property on the pewsham estate in chippenham ...
£259,950 Webbington Rd, Pewsham, Chippenham, Wiltshire, SN15
www.nestoria.co.uk

Local GP
The Lodge Surgery Lodge Road Chippenham Wiltshire SN15 3SY Tel: 0844 477 0919

The Red Lion Ghost
Reputed to be haunted by a 17th century woman called 'Florrie', murdered by her husband suspecting adulter and cast into a well.
The Red Lion Avebury, (01672) 539266

Calne

St Mary's School,
Calne, Wiltshire SN11 0DF
School Office 01249 857300
www.stmaryscalne.org

St Margaret's Preparatory School
Calne Wiltshire SN11 0DF
T: 01249 857220
www.isc.co.uk/
school_StMargaretsPreparatorySch
ool_Calne

Calne Woodlands Camera Club
The club meets every Monday
evening (except for Bank Holi-
days) at the Woodlands Social
Club, Station Road, Calne,
Wiltshire SN11 0JE Tel: 01249
813361
www.calnecc.co.uk/

Calne Town Council
Bank House The Strand
Calne Wiltshire
SN11 0EN
Tel: 01249 814000
www.calne.gov.uk/

Canal here. Here are Bowood House and Gardens, closed until 28th March, and Bowood Hill Golf Course. Sandy Hill and Berry Lane are neighbours. A novel curved footbridge high over the road, connecting the estate to farmland.

Calne Twinned with Charlieu in France. Lyneham and Wootton Bassett are neighbours. The Portmarsh Industrial Estate is in the vicinity. A number 55 bus serves this area, trundling past St Mary's, Calne. St Margarets Preparatory School is next to St Mary's GSA Independent School, which has a considerable reputation for academic achievement. A narrow medieval lane, Curzon Street, leads into the town centre. Free stay for two hours at the

Calne

substantial Co-op car park. And you cross a small stream, past 17th century cottages by the Holy Trinity Church, Parish of Calne and Proclamation Steps, where news was broadcast to the town.

Recording with Mike Rawle, Warden of the Church of St Mary Calne.

NJ How old is the Church?

MR About 1180, it's basically late Norman. We have dug up a tower house, foundation. This is a Norman nave, but we've had constant rebuilding over the centuries. Most of it is perpendicular outside. The original church would have been this nave.

NJ It's got a nice tower on it.

MR It has. The side aisle and traverse were built in the 1650s. The original

Capability Brown designed gardens at
Bowood House,
Bowood Estate,
Calne, Wiltshire SN11 0LZ
T: 01249 812102
Bowood House 11am - 5.30pm during the season
Bowood Grounds 11am - 6.00pm during the season
Temple Gate Coffee Shop - 10.30am to 6.00 pm
Adults (13 years and above) £10.00
Senior Citizens (60 years and over) £8.50
Juniors 5-12 years £8.00
Children 2-4 years £5.25
Family (max 2 adults) £30.00
www.bowood-house.co.uk

Pioneer of photography
Fox Talbot Museum
Lacock Abbey,
Lacock SN15 2LG
0124973 0459
Adult: £10.70 Child: £5.30
Family: £27.30 Group: £10.00
www.nationaltrust.org.uk/lacock/

Calne

Serviced Offices
Carlton Business Centre
Maundrell Road Porte Marsh
Calne Wiltshire
SN11 9PU
T: 01249 816222
www.carltonbusinesscentre.co.uk/

Calne Leisure Centre
White Horse Way
Calne Wiltshire
SN11 0SP
T: 01249 819160
info@calneleisure.co.uk
www.calneleisure.co.uk/

tower came crashing down and wiped out the end of the church. So there's a strange mixture of Norman and Georgian arches, in the same style.

NJ And 19th century stained glass?

MR Yes, we had two very active 19th century vicars, Guthrie and Duncan. Guthrie was very wealthy, and made a lot of changes. All the box pews were ripped out, to let light in, and he commissioned fresh stained glass.

NJ Wiltshire is a curious shape. Its centre is taken up with the Salisbury Plain, with strings of settlements on the edges and below.

MR Absolutely, and I think there's very little connection between the North and the East. In the North you have Swindon, which isn't really

Calne

part of Wiltshire. Then you have North Wiltshire: Wootton Bassett, Calne, ourselves, Westbury, Trowbridge. The plain cuts off the connection with Salisbury. The diocesan boundaries are very odd. If they were carving the county again, Salisbury would go into the area with Bournemouth and Hampshire. We certainly have a connection with Bath.

NJ Calne is known for St Mary's School, which has a great reputation.

MR John Duncan was instrumental in founding the school. But Guthrie was the revolutionary. He founded practically all the schools in the town, he made a huge input on this church. So much so that, when his successor Duncan came along, there was a schism in the church. Duncan

Calne Town Football Social Club
Bremhill View Calne Wiltshire
SN11 9EE
T: 01249 816716

Calne Cricket Club
Beversbrook Road Calne
Wilts SN1 19F

Spa Medical Centre
Snowberry Lane
Spa Medical Centre,
Melksham, SN12 6UN
T: 01225 709311

A Visual Arts College
The Corsham School
The Tynings Corsham
SN13 9DF
01249 713284

Avebury

Avebury stone circles are thought to have been constructed in neolithic times between 2500 to 2000 BC. The Beaker people, so called after their pottery, are thought to have played a major role in their formation

Opening times: Mid March to November 10.00 am - 5.30 daily Saturdays: 1.00pm - 4.30pm and Sundays 11.00am - 4.30pm Tel: +44 (0) 1672 539425 www.wiltshire-web.co.uk/ history/avebury

Wiltshire Walk

Silbury Hill, West Kennett Long Barrow, and the entry to Avebury via West Kennet Avenue. 4 miles, 1.5hrs-2.5hrs www.wiltshirewalks.co.uk/

The Red Lion Ghost

Reputed to be haunted by a 17th century woman called 'Florrie', murdered by her husband suspecting adulter and cast into a well.

The Red Lion Avebury, (01672) 539266

was the visionary, very much a 19th century mover and shaker, in the 1860s. The key family of Calne is the Lansdowne family. William Petty made the first map of Britain in Charles 1's time, and he founded the Lansdowne family. They own all the land around here, thousands of acres.

Avebury Ring

I'm looking at the Avebury Ring which is very impressive, standing flat stones planted upright around the field, where sheep are grazing contentedly. The ancient landmark is bordered by some 17th century Queen Anne properties. Avebury Manor and Gardens are nearby (National Trust, or £10 admission). The stones vary from, just emerging

Devizes

from the grass to nearly two metres height, and they form a perfect circle. Beside the field is a banked moat.

Devizes

Past Horton and Bishops Canning on the A361, near to Avebury. The light is dropping in this mild November afternoon, lending a silvery light to this rather lovely, gentle landscape. Arrive at Devizes past an industrial estate, with Lidl and B&Q superstores for local needs. I note Le Marchand Military Barracks here. The square block of a castle tower greets one entering the town lending an imposing aspect.

Proceeding along Northgate Street you find the Northgate Brewery and visitor centre. The council offices are

Devizes School
The Green
Devizes SN10 3AG
Tel: 01380 724886

Arts & Entertainment
Palace Cinema
19/20 Market Place,
Devizes,
Wiltshire
SN10 1JQ

The Athenæum Centre
18 - 20 High Street,
Warminster, BA12 9AE
Box Office and Information
01985 213891

Leisure Centre
Swimming pool, gym and fitness, juniors
Mon-Fri 7am-10pm, Sat 8am-5pm, Sun 8am-8pm
Southbroom Road, Devizes
Wiltshire, SN10 5AB
Telephone: 01380 734880

Devizes

Heritage Museum
41 Long Street, Devizes, Wiltshire SN10 1NS
01380 727369
www.wiltshireheritage.org.uk/
events/

Boat Sales
Devizes Marina Village
Horton Avenue Devizes
Wiltshire SN10 2RH
Tel: 01380 725300
www.devizesmarina.co.uk/

Devizes Reclamation
Car Breakers in Devizes
Devizes Reclamation Co Ltd
Hopton Estate, London Road
SN10 2EY
Devizes Wiltshire

a'Beckett's Vineyard
High Street Littleton Panell
Devizes SN10 4EN
T: 01380 816669
www.abecketts.co.uk

located at Beaufort. Here flows the Kennet and Avon Canal, and Caen Hill marina and locks. Horton, Rowde and Pouleshot are neighbouring villages. Foxhangers Marina services the water traffic of narrow boats and cruisers.

I pull up in Northgate Street for the town centre. First sight is the impressive Wadworth Brewery, favourite ale of Wiltshire (Wadworthshire). Past Devizes Literary and Scientific Institute into the market at the town centre, where you find The Gazette and Herald offices. It's a busy and lively thoroughfare; market day happens on Thursday.

The amusingly named Snuff Street Stalls sell everything from DVDs to electrical goods, household cleaners,

Martinslade . Sells Green .

fruit, fish, bread. An Italian Boutique and *'Mistral'* bravely keep fashion and style for the populace. The famous Shambles market is housed in a long arcade. Enticing aromas of food, sweet chicken kebabs being grilled on the street. *The Brittox* has M& Co, Spec Savers, and in the middle - fun for children - a giant multicoloured stack of helium balloons held somehow by a sole trader. *Ethnique Trading* has some interesting bespoke craft furniture.

Martinslade and Sells Green

Scattered settlements on the A365 towards Melksham. Sundry small industrial units and Victorian properties. The Three Magpies for hospitality, then into the fields, past a pig farm, on a silver pink winter's after-

Holt Dramatic Society
www.holtdrama.org.uk/

Courts Garden
Holt, near Bradford on Avon,
BA14 6RR
Telephone: 01225 782875
Open 11am-5.30pm
www.nationaltrust.org.uk/courts-garden/

The Tollgate Inn
Holt, Nr Bradford on Avon,
Wiltshire, BA14 6PX Tel 01225 782326
www.tollgateholt.co.uk

B&B Holt
The Old Stable House
www.theoldstablehouse.co.uk/

Church of St Katherine Holt
Church Street, Holt, Wiltshire,
BA14 6QA
www.stkatharinesholt.org.uk

The Shambles, Bradford On Avon

Riverside,walk, Bradford On Avon

Autumn leaves, Bradford On Avon

Bower Hill . Challymead .

Caen Hill Locks
Avon Road Devizes
Wiltshire SN10 1PR
Tel: +44 (0)1452 318000

Wadworth Real Cider at
The Three Magpies, Sells
Green, Seend, Wiltshire,
SN12 6RN.
Tel: (01380) 828389

Dairy Farmer
Fred Haines & Son, Little
Thornham Farm, Trowbridge
Rd., Seend, Melksham,
SN12 6PQ
(01380) 828284

noon. The Barge Inn is situated off this road at Seend.

Bowerhill

On the A365, widespread community of newish buidings. Bowerhill industrial estate is here. A number 14 bus serves this area.

Challymead

On the road to Bradford On Avon, just outside Melksham. Broughton Gifford is a neighbour. It is simply a cluster of a few properties on the main road, with no obvious amenities, so go shop in Melksham. Bradford is five miles away. A sparsely populated area with old nursery gardens, a farm.

Bradford On Avon .

Holt

A modern development of two/ three bed properties in Little Park, otherwise plain faced Victorian dwellings. It spreads on and on. For stocking up- Holt Superstore. The Old Ham Tree Inn introduces Holt village green, a triangle with a war memorial at its centre. Bradford is three miles away, Woolley Grange is nearby. Bath is in easy reach.

Bradford On Avon

Coming into Bradford the historic Moulton Bicycle Company is sighted and a musical museum. It is very picturesque, with Jacobean proper-ties in that cool Bath stone.

A volume of morning traffic pumping through the centre, forcing its way up unsuitably narrow lanes.

Wiltshire Music Centre
Ashley Road, Bradford on Avon, Wiltshire, BA15 1DZ
Box Office 01225 860100
www.wiltshiremusic.org.uk/

Swimming Pool
Station Approach, Bradford on Avon,
Wiltshire, BA15 1DF.
Telephone: 01225 862970.

Dine at
Ale and Porter
25 Silver Street
Bradford on Avon
BA15 1JZ
Tel: 01225 868 135
www.aleandporter.co.uk/

Bradford On Avon

Walkers are Welcome
Bradford on Avon is the first
assigned town in Wiltshire.
Enjoy the Macmillan Way and
Kennet and Avon Canal,
which pass through the town.
www.bradfordonavon.co.uk/
walkersarewelcome

Town Council
St Margaret's Hall, Bradford
On Avon
T: 01225 864240
www.bradfordonavontowncouncil.
gov.uk/

I divert into a new development in traditional styles apartments and town houses near to the river Avon; Upper Mill Residential Estate.

Parking not easy as a local market has helpfully colonised the short stay car park. Over a level crossing. Finally pull up in Church Street.

A Catholic church here, which gives onto the high street, with *The Dandelion* and *The Olive Tree*. Bradford is very up and down hill. Across the busy road into The Shambles, a little shopping precinct, fronted by the post office and a bookshop.

Here you can browse a coffee shop cum delicatessen with all sorts of Italian delicacies. A fruiterer spreads their produce on outdoor trestles, on the corner of Coppice Hill.

Farley Wick . Bathford .

At the end of Church Street finds a quiet riverside walk, the broad still water reflecting aspects of beautiful cream faced Georgian buildings and copper autumn tints of the tall trees.

Farley Wick

A small cluster on the Bath Road, just beyond Bradford on Avon. The road winds along beside a valley; woodlands for sale. Across the valley appears the spreading view of Bath.

Bathford

Near Bath, beside a broad valley, the village is tucked above the main road, with its church and a village community hall. Avondale RFC have their base here.

Anglo-Saxon Church
The Church of St.Laurence
AD700 at the centre of
Bradford on Avon

Bradford on Avon Health Centre
Station Approach
Bradford on Avon
Wiltshire BA15 1DQ
T: 01225 866611
www.boahc.co.uk/

National Archives
Explore Wiltshire and Swindon Archives
on UK archives network
www.nationalarchives.gov.uk/A2A/records.

Guide Price
Farm House with 4 bedrooms, 2 reception rooms, 2 bathrooms nr Salisbury Wilts. OIRO £1,750K Primelocation.com

Woolley Green . Staverton .

Woolley Green

On the Trowbridge Road, not far from Bradford on Avon, is hust a small settlement above the main route. I note the sign to Woolley Grange, a comfortable family run hotel in a fine Jacobean mansion, enjoyed on previous stays.

Staverton

A great concrete block of a building, signed *'Trapeze'*, introduces Staverton. A big disused factory. Up the hill past Staverton Racing Stables and the Old Bear Inn. Over a bridge and the community extends. A line of bungalows in Cockles Barton. Trowbridge is nearby on the B1036.

Trowbridge

Trowbridge

Nearly impossible to access, signage is terrible. Trailing for an hour around the perimeter: Marsh Road, Church Street, business centres, industrial units, turning right by the *Lion and Fiddle* for all routes. Trowbridge indicated ahead on the A361; the town centre shows up and vanishes, leading one into a maze of mis-directions, all leading into the suburb of New Town.

Trowbridge, the unitary authority of Wiltshire, has built itself an intricately defended fortress compound ringed by lavish and spectacular retail parks. The obscure signs confuse: I don't want Westbury, Warminster, Chippenham or Devizes; I want Trowbridge.

Town Council Reception
01225 765072 option 1
info@trowbridge.gov.uk

Tourist Information Centre
01225 765072 option 3
tic@trowbridge.gov.uk
www.trowbridge.gov.uk/

Sports Centre
Frome Road,Trowbridge,
Wiltshire, BA14 0DJ
01225 764342
www.dcleisurecentres.co.uk/
Centres/

Wiltshire College Trowbridge Campus
College Road · Trowbridge ·
Wiltshire BA14 0ES
T: 01225 766241
www.wiltshire.ac.uk/centres/
trowbridge/

Trowbridge

Urban Dance are a group of children and young adults between the ages of 4 and 17 years who attend a weekly session, run by volunteers and www.bjrs.eu/UrbanDance/

Country Hotel & Spa
Hilperton Rd, Trowbridge
01225 768336
www.fieldwayshealthhotel.co.uk

The Trowbridge Village Pump Festival takes place at Stowford Manor Farm in Wiltshire, one of the most picturesque settings in the country for an event of this type.
trowbridgefestival.com

Author commends
The Conigre Hotel.
Semington Road.
Melksham.
Wiltshire. SN12 6BZ /
T:01225 702229
www.theconigrehotel.co.uk/

Finally I take a white walled ramp to a rooftop car park, still in construction, over the Gateshead Shopping Centre. Next and all the big stores are here. In the coffee shop, mothers and buggies and boyfriends/husbands, passing time, a man bouncing baby on his knee.

Senior citizens rest with a long coffee and a slice of cake. I move on to check the Shires Shopping Mall over a walkway, with glimpses of the old town beyond. An attractive blue steeled glass roof of the atrium shelters flows of shoppers, browsing a marvellous array of fruit and veg; *Tailor Made* butchers beside *Superdrug, Poundland* asnd *Boswell's café*. It is enormous. The other end gives onto Fore Street, and the town.

Semington Turnpike . Seend .

The Semington Turnpike and Salt Store

A new development near Trowbridge; Great Hinton is off to the right, and then *The Strand* on the A365. A working farm with wrapped bales of hay and a pretty apple orchard. A water meadow feeling to this area.

A Jacobean property to let here by Philip O'Shea. The Lamb Inn for hospitality. Cleeve House is holding a craft fair nearby; Devizes and Seend are eight miles away.

Seend

A lovely 17th century red brick mansion, and other pretty white painted properties. A football pitch next to Cook's Close. Various attractive houses here. An old one with its flank windows bricked up, remind-

Light industrial
Workshops to let at Semington Turnpike
Kavanaghs.co.uk

Turnpike Foods Ltd
supplying delicatessens in Trowbridge
1-2 Semington Turnpike
Semington Trowbridge
Wiltshire BA14
Tel: 01380 870 758

Seend
The name of Seend is possibly derived from the old English word for sand, and it is clear that the ridge of greensand on which it lies, rising up out of the heavy marshy lands to north and south, attracted a settlement at an early date
www.seend.org.uk/history

Alton Priors, The Vale of Pewsey

Etchihampton, The Vale of Pewsey

Misty morning, Devizes

Honey Street . Woodborough .

Timber Yard
Honeystreet Sawmills Ltd
The Old Builders Wharf
Honeystreet Pewsey
Wiltshire SN9 5PS
T: 01672 851565

The Barge Inn
Favourite mooring for narrow
boat users on the Kennet and
Avon Canal. Great sausage
and mash, author sampled!
Honey Street
Wiltshire, SN12 6QB
01380 828230
www.bargeinnseend.co.uk

Crop Circles
'Woodborough is in the centre
of Crop Circle country and the
Barge Inn at Honey Street just
up the road is an international
focus for "croppies". Every
year several crop circles mys-
teriously appear overnight'
www.communigate.co.uk/wilts/
woodborough/

ing one of the avoidance of the window tax in the 18th century.

Honey Street and Woodborough

Villages located in the Pewsey Vale, in sight of the White Horse. A very-beautiful area, accessed with some difficulty by a long winding lane down from Great Overton near Marlborough.

Note a C of E school at Woodborough, a little community in deep countryside. This leads into Hilcott, small cottages beside the road. All on a long winding road going across the Pewsey Vale.

North Newnton

In the Pewsey Vale; has a corrugated hangar barn by a small lodge farmhouse in working land.

Upavon . West Chisenbury .

Past the Woodbridge Inn, Salisbury is eighteen miles away,

Upavon

On the road towards Amesbury, a picturesque settlement of delightful thatched cottages; one for sale by Carter Jonas. The Antelope Inn, obscured by a leafy vine. Widdington, in the vicinity, has a shooting club from March to August. Upavon has its own golf club. The sun is dropping on a warm November afternoon.

West Chisenbury

On the way to Amesbury; sparsely populated, just a hangar barn and a nice red brick 18th century residence. Compton is a neighbour. Plenty of bus stops imply a well served route to

Upavon History
'A Benedictine priory, a cell to Fontanelle abbey in France, was founded here in the time of Henry I. and was given, at the suppression of alien monasteries, to Ivychurch priory.
www.visionofbritain.org.uk/

Stay at
The George Hotel, High St, Amesbury, SP4 7ET
11.31 kilometers from West Chisenbury. Room prices starting from £45

The Church of All Saints
Chestnut Rise, Fittleton, Wiltshire SP4 9PZ
13th century, restored in 1903
More info at
www.britishlistedbuildings.co.uk/en-311005-church-of-all-saints-fittleton

Netheravon . Durrington .

All Saints Voluntary Aided CE Primary School High Street, Netheravon, Wiltshire, SP4 9PJ
T: 01980 670339

Dog and Gun, Netheravon, Wiltshire, SP4 9RQ
0871 951 1000

Netheravon holds a key place in the history of military aviation having had a hand in the birth of the RFC, the RAF, the Fleet Air Arm and the original Army Air Corps.
www.drumbeat.org.uk/netheravon.

Army Parachute Association Airfield Camp Netheravon Wiltshire SP4 9SF
www.netheravon.com/

Durrington C Of E (Controlled) Junior School Bulford Road Durrington SP4 8DL
Tel: 01980 652237
www.durrington-jun.wilts

Salisbury. *Hexton and Fittleton* located down an impenetrable track near Netheravon; one house sighted.

New Town

A settlement strung along the A345 to Salisbury; a bungalow here, a Victorian red brick there. Fifield is a neighbour.

Netheravon

A modern development down Court Farm Road-WSB Group to let. The old village is a ¼ mile to the left. A sign reads *Danger, Tanks Crossing Road*, obviously a site for military manoeuvres. Barbed wire mesh fences secure the area. Figheldean, a small cluster of houses, is just nearby.

Woodhenge . Amesbury .

Durrington

With Hackthorne as a neighbour, on the A345 to Amesbury. A big cemetery here. Sheep grazing and horses in a paddock. Fairly substantial, it has *Avonfields*, a new show home marketing suite. 1950s mock Tudor properties facing a new build estate of three/four bed properties.

Stonehenge Golf Driving Range is in the vicinity.

Woodhenge and Amesbury

A small cluster on the A345 to Amesbury. There is a Holiday Inn located at Soltice Park. It is right beside Amesbury, detached modernish houses bordering the routes to Salisbury or left to London and the A303. Boscombe Down and Buford are

Woodhenge and Amesbury
Woodhenge is a Neolithic site, probably built about 2300 BC, and was identified in 1925. The site was believed to consist of a central burial, surrounded first by six concentric rings of postholes, then by a single ditch and finally an outer bank, around 85 metres wide

Located 1.5 miles North of Amesbury, off A345, just South of Durrington
Free entry.
Site Telephone 0870 3331181

www.tourist-information-uk.com/woodhenge

Cawston

Strangers
'There are no strangers in
Wiltshire, just people that
you have yet to meet!'
from Cawston Community Portal
www.cawston.2da/ws

Antique bookcases in Cawston
Stocked by Hingstons of
Wilton, antique dealers.
Showroom: 36 North Street
Wilton Salisbury,
Wiltshire.SP2 0HJ
Tel: 01722 742263

Stonehenge
A344 Road, Amesbury,
Wiltshire SP4 7DE
01722 343834
Adult £7.80, Child (to 15)
£4.70, Family (2A,3C) £20.30
Open Mon-Sun 9.30am-4pm
Cafes, info-point, souvenir
shop, disabled facilities

along this way, but will be passing out of Wiltshire soon.

Saturday 14th January 2012
Cawston/Malmesbury
Driving towards Cawston on the way to Malmesbury, passing a Go-Kart operation located in a big black and white striped hangar building on the outskirts of the village.

Here is a new build development of Jacobean style three bed. properties. Manor Farm is here, there's a little parish church. Strakers is an agent for this area; Rodbourne and Foxley are neighbours. Entering the town past Malmesbury Primary Health Care Centre, NHS Trust, then down an incline past Avon Mills, over a small bridge to the town centre.

Malmesbury

A quaint high street, medieval, Malmesbury has a deep history going back to the seventh century. A passage called The *King's Walk* leading to steps downhill to the valley the town sits above, and an Inn *'The Smoking Dog'*, then come upon the Malmesbury Cross in the small open area of the centre, the great Abbey is sighted beyond.

Park by The Three Cups off the centre and take in the beautiful aspect of the church overlooking the spread of the valley in a frosty winter light.

A lovely 18th century dress in the window of Cotswold Stitchcraft. local services include Leonard Walker, Poulterer and Game Dealer; French Furniture, Miles Morgan Travel.

Local news
Events, classes, developments at Malmesbury Community Portal
www.malmesbury.com/

Zumba Classes at Malmesbury Athelston House, Mondays 8am.

Malmesbury Bridge Club
Athelstan House
Details tel: 01666 822380

Malmesbury Youth Centre
Telephone 07990 908550

Athelstan Museum,
Cross Hayes, Malmesbury, SN16 9BZ
01666 829258
www.athelstanmuseum.org.uk/

Malmesbury

Naked Gardeners

Malmesbury Abbey Gardens, the home of 'naked gardeners' Ian and Barbara Pollard.

'Admission to the gardens on a Clothes Optional Day does not require a visitor to be without their clothes. The opportunity is offered to anyone who so wishes to spend their time within the garden boundaries without their clothes. We are not a club requiring membership, do not have club facilities and offer simply the opportunity to visit the gardens without clothes and without comment.' *Ian and Barbara Pollard*
www.abbeyhousegardens.co.uk/

Market Cross

The Market Cross was built at the end of the 15th Century and was, according to a quote of the time "a place for poor folkes to stand when the rain cometh."

Malmesbury Town Council

Malmesbury Town Hall
Cross Hayes Malmesbury
Wiltshire SN16 9BZ
Telephone: 01666 822143
www.malmesbury.gov.uk/

The centre is very picturesque with main shopping leading away down the high street. You can brunch at '*The Whole* Hog' on the square, popular with locals, (the bangers and mash were recommended). Or choose a more formal setting of the prestigious Old Hotel next to the Abbey.

A civic square includes Malmesbury Town Hall, and the Potters Yard; a veterinary surgeon plus a smart glass fronted gallery and local cinema in Cross Hayes.

Enter the Abbey grounds by Birdcage Walk, and pause to take in its magnificent structure, the main body dates from 610AD, but no spire or Church Tower. The doorway, curved with intricate lattice work patterns of

Malmesbury

biblical episode. Look up to see the marvellous sculpture of a family of Saints.

In conversation with an Abbey Steward

"Good afternoon, how old is the Abbey?" "Very old, the earliest part though the Lych Gate dates from 610-AD. If you look at the map on the wall you'll see how much was lost. The spire fell through the roof in Henry VIII's time."

"We came through the main door, with its incredible decoration; very corroded now, but how it must have looked in the first place."

Wonderful illuminated volumes are on display, (reading the cabinet's description): "Draftsmen marked the layout before scribes copied the words with goose feather quills.

Malmesbury Art Society
Workshops are held at St Mary's Hall, Malmesbury SN16 0DS and run from 10 - 4 on a Saturday
Cost is £17/non-members, £15/members.
www.malmesburyartsociety.blogspot.com

Malmesbury Garden Club
The Club currently has a membership of over 200 and covers Malmesbury and the surrounding villages.
Talks are held monthly at the Malmesbury Town Hall from September to April inclusive. Annual events include a Spring Plant Sale, an August Bank Holiday show and the October Harvest Supper.
www.malmesburygardenclub.org.uk/

Malmesbury Tennis Club
Tetbury Hill Gardens
Tetbury Hill Malmesbury
SN16 9JP
www.malmesburytennisclub.co.uk/

Malmesbury

Their ink was a solution of oak apples, lamp black iron salt, applied with gold leaf - which is incredible. - burnished with bone, the powdered gold painted with diluted egg white. and mineral extracts. They even used stale urine and ear wax - unbelievable!

Amazingly fine work, the paper has warped but the volumes are in very good condition.

Coming out of Malmesbury one finds a recent development of traditionally styled homes in Chubb Close and Mynott Close. Malmesbury Business Centre is on the road going to Chippenham and Cirencester. Going owards Upper Minety and Minety and then to bypass Swindon back to the M4 motorway.

Brokenborough

Brokenborough in the up and down countryside beyond Malmesbury. A very small settlement surrounded by apple orchards, it's just on the county line by Gloucestershire.

Apart from farming, what work options out here? Cultivating organic produce for supply chains and niche store and home crafts. On the road to Minety I pass Charlton Business Park, which appears an attractive situation of old buildings, at the corner of a large private estate.

Along this way you find the impressive Rectory Hotel, gated in its own grounds.

Eastcourt Five miles away from Malmesbury. Settled and pleasantly attractive it includes a cluster of newish properties and comfortable

The Horse Guards Public House
Brokenborough, , SN16 0HZ
T: 01666 822 302

Office space in Brokenburgh
A business centre based within an attractive, listed property and has a variety of office space available to let.
www.yourcityoffice.com/uk-office-space-Wiltshire/serviced-offices-Brokenborough.

Angling nr Brokenborough
Bowds Pond T: 01793 740255
Operated by: Haydon Street Angling Society
www.waterscape.com/things-to-do/fishing/fisheries/

St John The Baptist Church Brokenborough
Built in 1248, located two miles from Tetbury near the county boundary with Gloucestershire.

Vale of Malmesbury

The Old Hotel and Lych Gate of Malmesbury Abbey

The King's Walk Malmesbury

Malmesbury Abbey

Malmesbury Abbey portal: A family of Saints

The Bell Inn, Swindon Old Town

A Wiltshire barn conversion

Upper Minety . Cricklade .

Avebury Manor
Reopened to the public following a major restoration supported by the BBC and National Trust. The 17th century mansion is featured in the BBC Television production *To The Manor Reborn*.

Avebury Manor and Winter Garden reopened 11 February until 31 October 2012. From 1st April last entry is 4.00pm. Open from Thursdays to Tuesdays (closed every Wednesday)
Entry is by timed ticket.
Avebury Museum
Gift Aid prices: Adult £4.90, Child £2.45, Family £13.45
www.nationaltrust.org.uk/
avebury/

Upper Minety For Sale
Situated at the end of a no through lane with views over the 15th century church is this character property. »»
£275K (Nestoria)

bungalows. A flock of sheep grazing and Robswood stables.

Upper Minety is set in delightful countryside in North Wiltshire, Minety Church, middling to new properties. No shop, no inn. Turn down Dog Trap Lane, behind a horse and trap. Note Home Farm Business Park, near to Minety.

Hornbury Hill, Minety and Cricklade
A higgledy scatter of bungalows and terraces spread over a wide area. For hospitality, *The Turnpike*. Council housing, and the *Vale of the White Horse Inn* on the outskirts of the village. An area of patchwork developments without a particular identity. Blakehill Farm Nature Reserve is here. Cricklade is accessed through a pair of white iron gates.

Hornbury Hill . Minety .

I follow the Purton Road into unfolding housing estates that border West Swindon. The town centre is well served: a practical working environment. Fairview Fields has a large crowded car park, indicating an industrial unit or superstore. Then out on the A419 with eleven miles to the M4. Neighbours are Castle Keep and Kempford, two miles away.

Swindon is an important commercial centre; ruling its own independent fiefdom.

Swindon

Coming into the old town having negotiated the massive commercial quarter that rings the centre.

Swindon is known as a major centre of business and enterprise; home to WH Smith Head Office, among

Kinch Coaches Ltd
Hornbury Hill Malmesbury
Wiltshire SN16 9QH
01666 860339

Minety CE Primary Sawyers
Hill Malmesbury Wiltshire
SN16 9QL Tel: 01666 860 257

Origin of Minety
The name Minety comes from 'mintie' or 'mintiea' (mint stream). There was a small steam a little to the west of the village.
www.history.wiltshire.gov.uk/community/

Wiltshire Studies
Wiltshire & Swindon History Centre Cocklebury Road Chippenham SN15 3QN

Cricklade Hotel Golf Club,
Common Hill,
Cricklade, SN6 6HA.
Telephone, 01793 750751

Swindon

Swindon Borough Council
Civic Offices
Euclid Street Swindon
SN1 2JH
www.swindon.gov.uk/

Swindon Museum and
Art Gallery
Bath Road Swindon SN1 4BA
Tel: 01793 466556
Open Wednesday to Saturday
from 10.00am to 5.00pm.
Admission free

The Swindon Card
Can be used at leisure facilities
and other council venues in
Swindon to gain discounted
prices.
www.swindon.gov.uk/lc/lc-
sportrec/lc-sportrec-booking/lc-
sportrec-booking-swindoncard/
Pages/lc-sportrec-booking-
swindoncard.aspx

Arts Centre
Devizes Road
Old Town Swindon SN1 4BJ
Box Office Tel: 01793 614837

others. I chance on Swindon Museum and Art Gallery, housed in a modest mid Victorian building.

Swindon Old Town is unpretentious, perhaps a touch dilapidated, with various local businesses in operation. Across the high street leads into Wood Street past the Country Coffee Shop.

A variety of interesting shops in this quiet Victorian quarter, dominated at No.20 by 'Kings', a trendy restaurant bar. Here is Old Town Hardware, with stacks of useful implements and buckets outside, then interesting and artful boutiques: on the corner is *Trousseau*, a pretty bridal wear service.

It leads out to a main road, and the imposing Goddard Arms. The city spreads away to Roughton and

Swindon Old Town

Devizes. Cornmarket House is at No.1 Market Square, where a 19th century church being deconstructed.

A stretch of common land walled in Charlotte Mews for dog walking. Here is the wonderful Bell Hotel Swindon, with an enormous model bell suspended before the premises. Newport Street has *Gilberts Fine Furniture*, which was established in 1866. An unruly, traffic strewn route, overlooked by the Co-operative Convenience Store. A No.11 bus serves the area.

Swindon is zoned as East and West, with continual busy through traffic. You can rent here for £575 per month, or purchase a freehold; 4 beds, two reception, for between £195K and £245K *(McFarlanes)*.

Butterfly World
Studley Grange Garden & Leisure Park, Hay Lane, Wroughton, Swindon, Wilts, SN4 9QT
01793 852 400
www.studleygrange.co.uk/ butterflyworld/

Swindon Designer Outlet,
Kemble Drive,
Swindon, Wiltshire, SN2 2DY,
Monday - Friday 10am - 8pm
Saturday 10am - 7pm
Sunday 10am - 5pm (larger stores open at 11am)
www.swindondesigneroutlet.com

Swindon College
North Star Avenue, Swindon, Wiltshire SN2 1DY
01793 491591
www.swindon-college.ac.uk

Swindon Town Football Club
The County Ground
County Road
Swindon Wiltshire SN1 2EU
T: 0871 876 1879
www.swindontownfc.co.uk/

Swindon

Local News
Events, discussions, offers, venues
www.swindonweb.com/

Cineworld
Shaw Ridge Leisure Park, Whitehall Way, Swindon SN5 7DN
0871 200 2000

Swindon Business Link
Emlyn Square, Swindon, Wilts SN1 5BP
0845 600 9966
https://
online.businesslink.gov.uk/

Oasis Leisure Centre
North Star Avenue
Swindon
SN2 1EP

Tel: 01793 445401

www.swindon.gov.uk/lc/
lc-sportrec/lc-sportrec-facilities/

The town gardens are a quarter of a mile from here.

Trekking towards Warminster, ten miles away, I come into West Ashton in attractive rural surroundings. The Westbury Trading Estate is here. By the road several truck stops with their caravan cafés; sun glinting on the broad flat plain, dotted with the occasional farm. Allan & Harris sells in this area.

Yarnbrook

Near to Warmister with Frome as a neighbour, Longs Arms, a Methodist chapel and a cute little terrace of 19th century white cottages. Lightly wooded countryside, the road sign says, *Beware Stags Crossing*. Then a church out in the fields. Heywood

Yarnbrook . Westbury .

House is here. Westbury and The White Horse Country Park is ahead.

Westbury

As food was not served the lady at the Crown Inn pointed me to her daughter's café, *Madam Butterfly*, just around the corner, which was very pleasant: two enormous Wiltshire sausages, mash, peas and gravy, with a Coke - £6.75 -good value. The town, has an imposing town hall - it has shades of Thomas Hardy and '*The Mayor of Casterbridge*'. Parking is easy and free. The buildings are Queen Anne to Regency. An attractive market town but very quiet at the time of visit. Then to Warminster along the high street, passing the The Westbury Community Centre and Westbury Residential Care Home.

West End Eastleigh Surgery, Westbury, BA13 3JD
01373 822807

Longs Arms Public House
Yarnbrook, Wiltshire,
BA14 6AB

Westbury White Horse
Located on Westbury Hill, Wiltshire, the Westbury White Horse is the oldest of the Wiltshire horses. Situated on Westbury Hill, with spectacular panoramic views of the surrounding countryside.
www.wiltshirewhitehorses.org.uk /westbury

Warminster

Warminster School
Church street, Warminster,
Wiltshire BA12 8PJ
01985 210100
www.warminsterschool.org.uk/

Warminster Maltings Ltd
Provides a range of malts,
adjuncts, extracts and brewing
ingredients
39 Pound Street
Warminster, Wiltshire
BA12 8NN UK
Tel: 01985 212014
www.warminster-malt.co.uk/

Warminster Saddle Club
Oxendene Stables, Oxendene,
Warminster BA12 0DZ
01985 213 925
www.warminstersaddleclub.

Local news and information
www.warminster-web.co.uk/

Senior citizens making very slow progress up the high street with walking sticks and frames. Upton Scudamore is a neighbour, located in smooth banked downland of middle Wiltshire.

Warminster

Arrived by a fine Church past Warminster School and Sixth Form Centre; school kids on their mid-day break. Buildings of great character; an interesting old canopied clock on the side of a building. *The White Hart Inn, The Baby Shop and Schooldays, DPS Exotics, Crème De La Cod*, (very witty). The high street rises uphill: *The Little Flower Shop, Johnsons Cleaners, Brooms and Skittles, The Bath Arms* a most imposing Inn, *Feta Feast, The Masons Arms*, and as usual a Thai restaurant.

Bishopstrow . Norton Bavant .

All occupying the historic thorough-fare of the old town centre. There is a feeling of substance and authority to Warminster.

Bishopstrow and Norton Bavant

Located in attractive surroundings beyond Warminster, surrouinded by the great ancient barrows of downs. Eighteen miles from Salisbury. Chitterne is four miles away, and there is the sign of army occupation here at Larkhill Barracks. Codford and Knook are neighbouring villages.

Upton Lavell

On the way to Salisbury, an old village in the hills. A horse trekking centre is here.

Bishopstrow Spa
Bishopstrow House Hotel and Spa Warminster Wiltshire BA12 9HH
01985 212312
www.bishopstrow.co.uk/

Local information
www.thediscdirectory.co.uk/sw/ba/bishopstrow/leisure/tourist-information

Clock Cottage
Eastleigh Wood Lane Bishopstrow, Warminster, Wiltshire BA127BE
Rooms from £75
www.bedandbreakfastuk.co.uk/clock-cottage/

Codford . Chitterne .

Upton Lovell Shaman Barrow

dates from the Early Bronze
Age, 1900-1700 BC.
www.wiltshireheritage.org.uk/

The Prince Leopold Inn
Upton Lovell
Warminster
Wiltshire BA12 0JP
01985 850460
www.princeleopold.co.uk/

The George Hotel
and Restaurant
Codford, Warminster,
Wiltshire
01985 850270

Noted Feature
The Round House at Chitterne
www.round-house.demon.co.uk

Codford and Chitterne

A rambling old mansion sighted, in a plain early 19th century style, before ghastly Gothic style hit in the weird Victorian era, convoluted and stuffy. Georgian and Regency are my preference. I pass along a road above a broad valley and panoramic vista of little villages and well cared for pasture land.

Bath Spa

Bath Abbey from York Street

Union Street colonnade, Bath

Pierrepont Street, Bath

Thermal Pool, Bath

Bath Spa

Bath Spa University
Newton Park,
Newton St Loe,
Bath, BA2 9BN
Telephone: (01225) 875875

The Roman Baths
Abbey Church Yard
Bath BA1 1LZ
Adult £12.25, Senior/F-T Student £10.75, Child £8, Family (2A+4C) £35
Open 9.30am-4.30pm
www.romanbaths.co.uk/

Top Tea Place Award
by UK Tea Guild 2010
The Jane Austen Centre Regency Tea Rooms
40 Gay Street Bath
BA1 2NT
Tel: +44 (0) 1225 443000
www.janeausten.co.uk/tearooms/

Walking Tours of Bath.

Bath Spa 14th December 2011
Finally arrived at Bath Spa after the train broke down at Chippenham, and walking away from the station.

Fine Georgian buildings remind one that, in the 18th century, fashionable society colonised Bath, taking advantage of its warm thermal springs of natural waters from Roman times, and the opportunity to mix and party in its salons and assembly rooms. Jane Austen cast her beady eye on its comings and goings. The black coated Victorians, arrived from another planet in the 1840s, and swept remnants of that pleasure loving, sometimes dissolute, but very entertaining society, firmly away.

Bath Spa

Past the law courts one comes upon Bath Abbey, overlooking the elegant public gardens laid out below the bridge. Beyond one can see barges moored on the banks of the river Avon. Here is The Abbey Hotel and Ale House.

On the surrounding hills are sihjted elegant terraces of period properties. The streets are cobbled in fan- shaped patterns, the buildings are all faced with a creamy sandstone particular to the city. Entering the main shopping area in Southgate Street, a junction of five thoroughfares.

Lunch at the Pump Room in Bath, a high sided assembly room from the 18th century. A party of Japanese graduates at tea, looks splendid in their mortar boards and black gowns

A free service provided daily (Sunday - Friday 10.30 & 14.00, Sat 10.30), tours leave from outside the Abbey Churchyard entrance to the Pump Room. May to September. Led by Mayor of Bath Honorary Guides
www.visitbath.co.uk/travel-and-maps/mayor-of-bath-honorary-guides-p43001

Boat tours in the Pulteney Princess
Tickets: Henry Street, Pulteney Bridge,Bath,BA1 1EE, BA2 4
07791 910 650

The Royal Hotel,
Manvers Street, Bath BA1 1JP
T: 0844 682 6080
www.royalhotelbath.co.uk/

Bath PLUSBUS ticket
gives you unlimited bus travel on participating operators' services, around the whole urban area of Bath city
www.plusbus.info/bath-spa-plusbus

Bath Spa

The Riverside Inn The Shallows
Bath BS31 3EZ Rooms From:
£70. The Riverside Inn is situated just off of the A4 which
connects Bath and Bristol
www.bedandbreakfasts.co.uk/

Bath Abbey Bookshop
12 Kingstone Buildings Bath
BA1 1LT
T: 01225 303315

Batheaston Medical Centre
Coalpit Road Batheaston Bath
T 01225 858128

Hole in the Wall
16 George Street Bath
T 01225 425242

Duck & Punt
Bathford Bath
T 01225 859847

Terrace Restaurant Jolly's
7-14 Milsom Street Bath
T 01225 462811

slashed with blue and yellow.

At one end is a tall grandfather's clock, and 18th century portraits of local dignitaries and ladies. A piano provides a pleasant background for the steady and continuous flow of international visitors.

Out in Union Street under a colonnaded cover a brass band performs Christmas hymns. The street includes numerous designer shops, Monsoon, Paul Smith, and in Old Bond Street the bespoke tailor Christopher Barry. Gieves and Hawkes announce seasonal reductions. Here is the aptly named Quiet Street, with a goldsmiths. I cross over to explore Milton Place, a newly developed walkway of specialist shops and *Jamie's Italian* brasserie. The arcade is

Bath Spa

A boutique gallery of decorative glass-ware, with artists' hand blown vessels in brilliant tints of red, green, yellow and ultramarine. A modish store of Alessi kitchenware, in attractive retro designs-chose a pair of tall plastic cocktail beakers with 1950s graphics, added to a bulging bag of purchases.

Then exploring the historic covered Guildhall market, here since the early medieval times; burnt down and reconstituted in the 19th century.

All sorts of treasures here: a vendor of cured hams and meats; colourful knit-wear, bags and shawls; jars of Bath humbugs in a wonderful candy store; favourite destination for squeaking excited children. You fill a bag with multicoloured sweets which is weighed at the till.

The Pump Room Restaurant
Open daily for morning coffee from 9.30am until 12.00, and lunch from 12.00 - 2.30pm. Afternoon tea is served between 2.30pm and 5pm, last orders 4.00pm. Reservations: 01225 444477

The Roman Baths
Abbey Church Yard
Bath BA1 1LZ

Southgate Street, Bath

Walkway above the Thermal Spa, Bath

Royal Crescent, Bath

Milsom Street, Bath

Noth Parade Bath

Bath Spa

Bath 2 14ᵗʰ February 2012

Walking down from Royal Crescent in Queen's Parade and appreciating the tall backs of Georgian properties of The Circus, the long informal gardens stretching down to a pretty tree lined avenue; quiet back lane to the city centre. Neraby the Assembly Rooms include a Fashion Museum; with the Jane Austen Museum in the vicinity

Properties for sale between £380K for a two bed apartment, near the Circus, to £2.5 million for a Regency mansion in this quarter, or Camden Crescent further up the hill (a steep walk). Discover *Paxton &Whitfield*, the historic cheesemaker – it has a historic round of Stilton on display in the window. The walkway descends in easy levels

Guildhall Market
'Surviving from the 18th century is the 'Nail', a table on which market transactions took place, hence the saying, 'pay on the nail'.
High Street Bath BA2 4AW
www.visitbath.co.uk/shopping/

Fashion Museum
January - February 10.30 - 16.00
March - October 10.30 - 17.00
November -December 10.30 - 16.00
Adult £7, Senior £6.75, Ch £5.50, Family 2x4 £21.
Bath Assembly Rooms,
Bennett St, Bath, BA1 2QH
01225 477173
www.museumofcostume.co.uk/

Bath Spa

American Museum
Cl Mon, Open at 12 noon all
other days. Closed at 5.00pm
The Museum, grounds, café
and retail outlets all open at
12noon.
Adult £9, Conc £8, Ch £5,
Family (2x2) £24
Claverton Manor,
Bath BA2 7BD
01225 460 503
www.americanmuseum.org

Jane Austen Centre
40 Gay Street, Queen Square,
Bath BA1 2NT
01225 443000
www.janeausten.co.uk/

to Milsom Street, with individual shops to delay the journey; and back to the cleverly integrated Milsom Street Arcade with its cboutiques and courtyard cafés.

Bath Abbey was built in 1553 and contains a fine perpendicular nave with Tudor stained glass. Around the back is Abbey Green; a pretty Regency square, which includes a *Tea Shoppe*, the *Bath Bun Bakery*, *'Bijoux Beads'*, and the *Crystal Palace Inn* .

This leads to Southgate Street: and stores including *Superdrug, Top Shop*, and a brand new *Urban Outfitters*, a cool environment with the latest 'must have' trend fashions.

Buses stop at the bottom of Southgate Street, going to outlying districts and Bath University campus.

Bath Spa

Then a visit to the Roman Baths adjacent to the Pump Room; a rather marvellous and extensive restoration of the ancient thermal spa of natural hot spings enjoyed by the upper echelons of Roman colonial society.

Relics include preserved footwear and utensils; locks, nails, tools, coins, glassware and jewellery, with magnificent heads and figures of the Gods and Goddesses revered by the populace.

An intriguing display of Roman citizens' complaints enscribed on metal scraps, addressed to the Gods for reparation: pained by a stolen cloak or purse, or some other minor injury. Then back to the street to enjoy the lively action of this highly individual and spirited city.

Author recommends
Royal Crescent Luxury Hotel and Spa, 16 Royal Crescent, Bath BA1 2LS
01225 823333
www.royalcrescent.co.uk

Badminton Horse Trials
Three Day Equestrian Event
Badminton, Gloucestershire
GL9 1DF
01454 218272
www.badminton-horse.co.uk/

Bath Sports and Leisure Centre
North Parade Road,
Bath BA3 4ET
www.aquaterra.org/bath-sports-and-leisure-centre

Trowbridge Town Centre

Wiltshire Directory

Local services and useful addresses

Wiltshire Directory

Accommodation

Move Estate Agent & Letting Agents
67, Market Place, Warminster, Wiltshire,
BA12 9AZ
T: 01985 212 729

Kingston Estate Agents
11, High Street, Melksham,
Wiltshire, SN12 6JR
T: 01225 709 115

Arundell James Estate Agents
London House, High Street,
Tisbury, Salisbury, Wiltshire, SP3 6HA
T: 01747 871 234

Architects

Wyvern Architects
2, Marlborough Road, Swindon,
Wiltshire, SN3 1QY
T: 01793 574 949

Julian Taylor Chartered Architects
1, Mill Lane, Cherhill, Calne, Wiltshire,
SN11 8XS
T: 01249 816 055

Colin Johns Architect
27, St Margarets Street,
Bradford-On-Avon,
Wiltshire, BA15 1DN
T: 01225 868 037

Auctioneers

Southern Counties Auctioneers
The Livestock Market, Netherhampton Road,
Netherhampton, Salisbury, Wiltshire, SP2 8RH
T: 01722 340 041

Netherhampton Sale Rooms
The Livestock Market, Netherhampton Road,
Netherhampton, Salisbury, Wiltshire, SP2 8RH
T: 01722 342 045

Jubilee Auction Rooms
Unit D1, Fordbrook Business Center,
Marlborough Road, Pewsey,
Wiltshire, SN9 5NU
T: 01672 562 012

Chippenham Auction Rooms
St Mary Street, Chippenham,
Wiltshire, SN15 3JJ
T: 01249 446 300

Bakers

Reeve The Baker Ltd
6A, West Street, Wilton,
Salisbury, Wiltshire, SP2 0DF
T: 01722 742 539

The Old Bakery
15, High Street, Melksham,
Wiltshire, SN12 6JY
T: 01225 708 502

Marshall Bakery
3, Borough Fields Shopping Centre,
Wootton Bassett, Swindon,
Wiltshire, SN4 7AX
T: 01793 852 668

Myloaf
3, Martingate, Corsham,
Wiltshire, SN13 0HL
T: 01249 715 029

Wiltshire Directory

Banks

Barclays Bank Plc
66, Market Place, Chippenham,
Wiltshire, SN15 3JA
T: 0845 755 5555

Lloyds Tsb Bank Plc
125, High Street, Marlborough,
Wiltshire, SN8 1LU
T: 0845 300 0000

Santander
4, St Johns Street, Devizes, Wiltshire,
SN10 1BP
T: 0845 765 4321

The Royal Bank Of Scotland Plc
14, Minster Street, Salisbury,
Wiltshire, SP1 1TP
T: 01722 339 323

Halifax Plc
14, High Street, Westbury,
Wiltshire, BA13 3BW
T: 01373 826 851

Builders

Bodman Builders
43, The Street, Cherhill, Calne,
Wiltshire, SN11 8XR
T: 01249 816 932

Clark Builders
52, The Croft, Trowbridge,
Wiltshire, BA14 0RN
T: 01225 752 961

Building Societies

Nationwide Building Society
40A, Fore Street, Trowbridge,
Wiltshire, BA14 8EJ
T: 0845 266 1494

Stroud & Swindon Building Society
36, Market Street, Bradford-On-Avon,
Wiltshire, BA15 1LL
T: 01225 863 720

Portman Building Society
2-4, Church Street, Melksham,
Wiltshire, SN12 6LS
T: 0845 266 0593

Britannia Building Society
5, Market Place, Chippenham,
Wiltshire, SN15 3HD
T: 01538 399 399

Bus Services

Minerva Travel
The Laurels, Shurnhold House, Shurnhold,
Melksham, Wiltshire, SN12 8DG
T:: 01225 700 552

Coach Style
2 Horsedown Cottage, Horsdown,
Nettleton, Chippenham, Wiltshire,
SN14 7LN
T: 01249 782 224

Hunts Of Salisbury
Rockbourne Road, Coombe Bissett,
Salisbury, Wiltshire, SP5 4LP
T: 01722 718 851

Wiltshire Directory

Elite Limousines
12, Corfe Road, Melksham,
Wiltshire, SN12 6BQ
T: 01225 700 658

Business Centres

Windmill Hill Business Park,
Whitehill Way, Swindon,
Wiltshire, SN5 6PB
T: 01235 862 601

Hilltop Business Park,
Devizes Road, Salisbury,
Wiltshire, SP3 4UF

Dunkirk Business Park,
Dunkirk Business Park, Frome Road,
Southwick, Trowbridge, Wiltshire,
BA14 9NL

Butchers

Kingman Traditional Butchers
3-7, High Street, Amesbury, Salisbury,
Wiltshire, SP4 7ET
T: 01980 622 155

Leonard Walker Family Butchers
1, Market Cross, Malmesbury, Wiltshire,
SN16 9AS
T: 01666 822 132

Sumbler Bros
11, London Road, Marlborough, Wiltshire,
SN8 1PH
T: 01672 512 185

Vale Of Pewsey Butchers
6, High Street, Pewsey,
Wiltshire, SN9 5AQ
T: 01672 562 129

J E Fry & Son
Yew Tree Farm, South Street, Broad
Chalke, Salisbury, Wiltshire, SP5 5DH
T: 01722 780 203

Chemists

Shaunaks Ltd
Beechfield Road, Corsham,
Wiltshire, SN13 9DL
T: 01249 712 000

Rowland's Pharmacy
St Ann Street, Salisbury,
Wiltshire, SP1 2PT
T: 01722 411 775 82

Lloyds Pharmacy Ltd
High Street, Malmesbury,
Wiltshire, SN16 9AU
T: 01666 822 157 28

Cooperativee Pharmacy
High Street, Calne,
Wiltshire, SN11 0BS
T: 01249 812 506 13

Boots Stores Ltd
Penhill Drive, Swindon,
Wiltshire, SN2 5HN
T: 01793 723 534 257

Wiltshire Directory

Chippernham Family Health Centre
Goldney Avenue, Chippenham,
Wiltshire, SN15 1ND
T: 01249 653 184

Calne Family Health Centre
Broken Cross, Calne,
Wiltshire, SN11 8BN
T: 01249 812 821

Creches

Westgate Nursery School & Creche
82, Cricklade Road,
Highworth, Swindon,
Wiltshire, SN6 7BL
T: 01793 861 268

Sparklers Pre School
Shearwood Road,
Peatmoor, Swindon, Wiltshire, SN5 5DL
T: 01793 875 777 1

Silly Billys Mobile Creche

16, The Ridings, Kington St Michael,
Chippenham, Wiltshire, SN14 6JG

T: 01249 750 127

Delicatessens

Maple's Delicatessen
4, The Shambles, Bradford-On-Avon,
Wiltshire, BA15 1JS
T: 01225 862 203

The Deli at Corsham
18A, High Street, Corsham,
Wiltshire, SN13 0ES
T: 01249 716 091

The Polish Deli
Flat, St Georges Works, Silver Street,
Trowbridge, Wiltshire, BA14 8AA
T: 01225 761 268

Dentists

Wilton Dental Practice
16, North Street, Wilton,
Salisbury, Wiltshire, SP2 0HE
T: 01722 742 100

Dental Access Centre
Chippenham Community Hospital, Row-
den Hill, Chippenham,
Wiltshire, SN15 2AJ
T: 01249 456 633

Tisbury Dental Centre
Pump House, High Street,
Tisbury, Salisbury, Wiltshire,
SP3 6HD
T: 01747 870 743

Ferndale Dental Clinic
8, Estcourt Street, Devizes,
Wiltshire, SN10 1LQ
T: 01380 725 225

Wiltshire Directory

Doctors

Home Ground Surgery
North Swindon Practice
Thames Avenue, Swindon,
Wiltshire, SN25 1QQ

Porton Surgery
T: 01980 611 060
32, Winterslow Road, Porton,
Salisbury, Wiltshire, SP4 0LR
T: 0844 499 6631

Endless Street Surgery
72, Endless Street, Salisbury,
Wiltshire, SP1 3UH
T: 01722 336 441

Smallbrook Surgery
The Avenue, Warminster,
Wiltshire, BA12 8QS
T: 01985 846 700

Rowden Medical Partnership
Rowden Hill, Chippenham,
Wiltshire, SN15 2SB
 T: 01249 444 343

St James Surgery
Gains Lane, Devizes,
Wiltshire, SN10 1QU
T: 0844 477 8648

Electricians

Kennet Electrical Contractors Ltd
50, Kittyhawk Close, Bowerhill,
Melksham, Wiltshire, SN12 6QF
T: 01225 899 341

Adams Of Bath
81, Norbin, Box, Corsham,
Wiltshire, SN13 8JJ
T:01255 460 460

Accolade Electrical Ltd
8, Comfrey Close, Trowbridge,
Wiltshire, BA14 0XP
T: 01225 769 800

Moore Of Devizes Maintenance Ltd
8, Hartfield, Devizes, Wiltshire, SN10 5JH
T: 01380 720 033

Estate Agents

Davis & Latcham
43, Market Place, Warminster,
Wiltshire, BA12 9AZ
T: 01985 846 985

Madison Oakley Estate Agents
31, Shaftesbury Road,
Bath, Avon, BA2 3LJ
T: 01225 829 040

Cooper & Tanner
48-50, Market Place, Warminster,
Wiltshire, BA12 9AN
T: 01985 215 579

Mckillop & Gregory
44, Castle Street, Salisbury,
Wiltshire, SP1 3TS
T: 01722 414 747

Wiltshire Directory

Kavanaghs
13, High Street, Melksham,
Wiltshire, SN12 6JY
T: 01225 706 860

Farm Shops

Everleigh Farm Shop Ltd
The Old Rectory, Everleigh,
Marlborough, Wiltshire, SN8 3EY
T: 01264 850 344

Bird & Carter Farm Shop
Chilhampton Farmhouse,
Warminster Road, Wilton,
Salisbury, Wiltshire, SP2 0AB
T: 01722 744 177

Fosseway Fruits
Westwood Farm, Rode Hill, Colerne,
Chippenham, Wiltshire, SN14 8AR
T: 01225 743 533

Bison Centre
Bush Farm, West Knoyle,
Warminster, Wiltshire, BA12 6AE
T: 01747 830 263

Furniture (Antique)

Avon Antiques
25-27, Market Street, Bradford-On-Avon,
Wiltshire, BA15 1LL
T: 01225 862 052

Salisbury Antique Market
37, Catherine Street, Salisbury,
Wiltshire, SP1 2DH
T: 01722 326 033

Hingstons Of Wilton
36, North Street, Wilton,
Salisbury, Wiltshire, SP2 0HJ
T: 01722 742 263

Granny's Attic
The Citadel, Bath Road, Chippenham,
Wiltshire, SN15 2AB
T: 01249 715 327

Irene Nicholls
56, High Street, Malmesbury,
Wiltshire, SN16 9AT
T: 01666 823 089

Furniture (Modern)

Cloudberry Interiors
15, Church Street, Trowbridge,
Wiltshire, BA14 8DW
T: 01225 755 151

Mark Wilkinson Furniture Ltd
The Hopton Workshop, Hopton Road,
Hopton Road,Hopton Park Industrial
Estate, Devizes, Wiltshire,
T: 01380 730 186

Donal Channer & Co
50-52, Tower Hill, Dilton Marsh,
Westbury, Wiltshire, BA13 4DA
T: 01373 824 895

Courtyard Garden
Cross Keys Chequer, Salisbury,
Wiltshire, SP1 1EL
T: 01722 341 777

Wiltshire Directory

Garden Centres

Nurdens Garden Centre
Crudwell Road, Malmesbury,
Wiltshire, SN16 9JL
T: 01666 822 809

Court Farm
Court Farm, 6, Quakers Walk,
Goatacre, Calne, Wiltshire, SN11 9JQ
T: 01249 760 440

Trowbridge Garden Centre
288, Frome Road, Trowbridge, Wiltshire,
BA14 0DT
T: 01225 763 927

The Walled Garden Nursery
Brinkworth House, Brinkworth,
Chippenham, Wiltshire, SN15 5DF
T: 01666 826 637

Golf Clubs

Rushmore Golf Club
Phone number: 01725 516 391
Rushmore Park, Tollard Royal, Salisbury,
Wiltshire, SP5 5QB

Chippenham Golf Club
Phone number: 01249 652 040
Malmesbury Road, Langley Burrell, Chip-
penham, Wiltshire, SN15 5LT

The Bowood Hotel Spa & Golf & Country Club
Bowood House, Bowood, Calne,
Wiltshire, SN11 0LZ
T: 01249 822 228

Health Clubs

Curves Fitness
52A Fisherton Street
Salisbury
Wiltshire SP2 7RB
T: 01722 340 093

The Pink Gym
Avebury House, Stonehill Green,
Westlea, Swindon, Wiltshire, SN5 7HB
T:07887 698 073

Bodytech
1-2 Elmcross Business Park
Bradford-On-Avon
Wiltshire BA15 2AY
T:01225 865 704

Devizes Sports Club
Stourton London Road
Devizes Wiltshire SN10 2DL
T:01380 729 652

Leisure Centres

Castle Place Leisure Centre
Levela 5A, Multi Storey Car Park, Castle
Place, Trowbridge, Wiltshire, BA14 8AL
T: 01225 762 711

Calne Leisure Centre Ltd
White Horse Way, Calne,
Wiltshire, SN11 0SP
T:01249 819 160

Wiltshire Directory

Cricklade Leisure Centre
Stones Lane
Cricklade Swindon
Wiltshire SN6 6JW
T: 01793 750 011

Libraries

Salisbury Library
Market Walk
Salisbury
Wiltshire SP1 1BT
T: 01722 330 606

Purton Library
Purton Library, 1, High Street, Purton,
Swindon, Wiltshire, SN5 4AA
T: 01793 770 870

Melksham Library
4B, Lowbourne, Melksham,
Wiltshire, SN12 7DZ
T: 01225 702 039

Trowbridge Library
Mortimer Street
Trowbridge
Wiltshire BA14 8BA
T: 01225 761 171

Chippenham Library
Timber Street
Chippenham
Wiltshire SN15 3EJ
T: 01249 650 536

Local Authorities

Chippenham Town Council
Town Hall
High Street Chippenham
Wiltshire SN15 3ER
T: 01249 446 699

Trowbridge Town Council
Civic Hall
St Stephens Place
Trowbridge
Wiltshire BA14 8AH
T: 01225 765 072

Swindon Town Council
Grange Park Way
Grange Park
Swindon
Wiltshire SN5 6HN
T: 01793 874 224

Museums

The National Trust
Mompesson House, The Close,
Salisbury, Wiltshire, SP1 2EL
T 01722 335 659

*The Rifle Berkshire
& Wiltshire Museum*
58 The Close
Salisbury
Wiltshire SP1 2EX
T: 01722 419 419

Wiltshire Directory

Chippenham Museum & Heritage Centre
9-10, Market Place, Chippenham,
Wiltshire, SN15 3HF
T: 01249 705 020

The Phillips Countryside Museum
Brokerswood House
Brokerswood Westbury
Wiltshire BA13 4EH
T:01373 822 238

Plumbers

L S P Gas Services
126, Wyke Road, Trowbridge,
Wiltshire, BA14 7NT
T: 01225 350 052

AWS Plumbing Ltd
91 North Street
Calne
Wiltshire SN11 0HJ
T: 01249 817 913

Merrett J Plumbing Heating
78, Downlands Road, Devizes,
Wiltshire, SN10 5EF
T: 01380 730 001

Home Engineering
29, Shaw Hill, Shaw, Melksham,
Wiltshire, SN12 8EU
T: 01225 707 156

Restaurants

Angelo's Restaurant
24, Milford Street, Salisbury,
Wiltshire, SP1 2AP
T: 01722 502 191

Olive Tree
3, Beach Terrace, Calne,
Wiltshire, SN11 0RD
T: 01249 812 508

Isola Bella
2A, Long Street, Devizes,
Wiltshire, SN10 1NJ
T: 01380 724 400

Whole Hog
8, Market Cross, Malmesbury,
Wiltshire, SN16 9AS
T: 01666 825 845

Riding Schools

Hampsley Hollow Riding Centre
Heddington, Calne,
Wiltshire, SN11 0PP
T: 01380 850 333

Richard Pitman Bloodstock
Woodlands Farm, Witcha, Ramsbury,
Marlborough, Wiltshire, SN8 2HQ
T: 07976 618 865

Riding For The Disabled
Pembroke Centre, Netherhampton,
Salisbury, Wiltshire, SP2 8PJ
T: 01722 744 822

Wiltshire Directory

Marden Grange Livery Stables
69, The Street, Marden, Devizes,
Wiltshire, SN10 3RQ
T: 01380 840 010

Sailing Clubs

West Wilts Youth Sailing Association
23 Fairdown Avenue
Westbury
Wiltshire BA13 3HS

Whitefriars Sailing Club
Orion House
The Old Brickyard
North End Ashton Keynes
Swindon Wiltshire SN6 6QR
T: 01285 861 670

Schools (Primary)

Winterbourne Earls C of E
Salisbury Wiltshire
SP4 6HA
T: 01980 611 356

Grove Primary
Hazel Grove
Trowbridge Wiltshire BA14 0JG
T: 01225 755 242

Schools (Secondary)

Melksham Oak Community School,
Bowerhill, Melksham,
Wiltshire, SN12 6QZ
T: 01225 792700

Wansdown Community School
Woodcock Road
Warminster Wiltshire
BA12 9DR
T: 01985 215 551

St Laurence School
Ashley Road
Bradford-On-Avon
Wiltshire
BA15 1DZ
T: 01225 309500

The John of Gaunt School
Wingfield Road
Trowbridge
Wiltshire BA14 9EH
T: 01225 762637

Schools (Independent)

Salisbury Cathedral School
1, The Close, Salisbury, Wiltshire, SP1 2EQ
T: 01722 555 300

Marlborough College
Marlborough, Wiltshire, SN8 1PA
T: 01672 892 200

Dauntsey's School
The Sanitorium, Dauntsey School, High
Street, West Lavington, Devizes, Wiltshire,
SN10 4HE T: 01380 814 500

Stonar School Ltd
Coombe Lane, Atworth, Melksham,
Wiltshire, SN12 8NT
T: 01225 701 740

Wiltshire Directory

Sports Clubs

Trowbridge Cricket & Sports Club
1,Timbrell Street, Trowbridge,
Wiltshire, BA14 8PL
T: 01225 752 538

Chippenham Sports Club
15, Bristol Road, Chippenham,
Wiltshire, SN15 1NH
T: 01249 652 867

Salisbury & South Wiltshire Sports Club
Wilton Road, Salisbury,
Wiltshire, SP2 9NY
T: 01722 327 108

Swindon School Of Gymnastics
1, Sedgebrook, Swindon,
Wiltshire, SN3 6EY
T: 01793 633 913

Surveyors

Smiths Gore
8A, High Street, Marlborough,
Wiltshire, SN8 1AA
T: 01672 529 050

Whitmarsh Lockhart
Lancaster House, Edison Park,
Edison Park,Hindle Way,
Swindon, Wiltshire, SN3 3RT
T: 01793 541 000

Jonathan Shortt Commercial
Montecello Farm House, Devizes Road,
Potterne, Devizes, Wiltshire, SN10 5LN
T: 01380 721 101

Index

OXFORDSHIRE

A COUNTY GUIDE

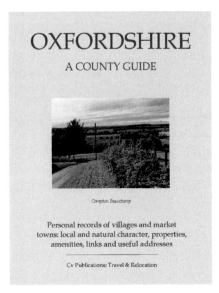

Compton Beauchamp

Personal records of villages and market towns: local and natural character, properties, amenities, links and useful addresses

Cv Publications: Travel & Relocation

ISBN 978-1908419-06-4

BUCKINGHAMSHIRE

A COUNTY GUIDE

Janet Barber

The Vale of Aylesbury

Records of villages and market towns: the properties, amenities, links and useful addresses

Cv Publications: Travel & Relocation

ISBN 978-1908419-09-5

GLOUCESTERSHIRE

A COUNTY GUIDE

Sarah James

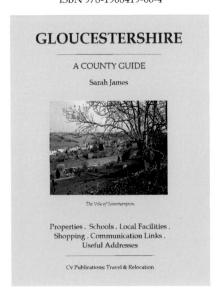

The Vale of Severnhampton

Properties . Schools . Local Facilities . Shopping . Communication Links . Useful Addresses

Cv Publications: Travel & Relocation

ISBN 978-1908419-07-1

CORNWALL

A COUNTY GUIDE

Nicholas James

Polruan

A personal record of over one hundred villages and market towns: the properties, amenities, links, maps and useful addresses

Cv Publications: Travel & Relocation

ISBN 978-1908419-10-1

NORFOLK

A COUNTY GUIDE

Records of over one hundred villages and market towns. Local character. Properties. Schools. Amenities. Services and communication links.

Cv Travel & Relocation

ISBN 978-1908419-01-9

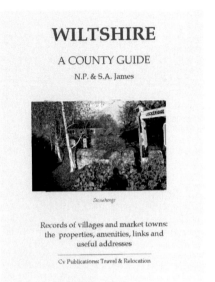

WILTSHIRE

A COUNTY GUIDE

N.P. & S.A. James

Stonehenge

Records of villages and market towns: the properties, amenities, links and useful addresses

Cv Publications: Travel & Relocation

ISBN 978-1908419-12-5

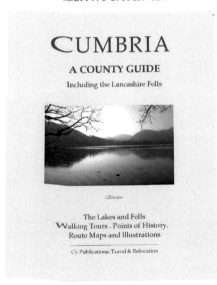

CUMBRIA

A COUNTY GUIDE

Including the Lancashire Fells

Ullswater

The Lakes and Fells
Walking Tours . Points of History.
Route Maps and Illustrations

Cv Publications: Travel & Relocation

ISBN 978-1908419-32-3

'A useful guide' *(Oxfordshire)*
Susan Crewe, Editor, House and Garden

'This assisted our own research for a new place to live' *Philip and Jessica (Gloucestershire)*

'I have enjoyed finding out about all the hidden villages.' *Becky (Buckinghamshire)*

'Refreshed our love of Cornwall' *Jennifer and Martin (Cornwall)*

'A comprehensive exploration' *Paul (Norfolk)*

'Magical journey' *Becky and Martin (Wiltshire)*

Malmesbury, Wiltshire

ART . WORK . TRAVEL . HISTORIES

Cv Publications . 10 Barley Mow Passage .
Chiswick . London . W4 4PH UK
Tel: +44(0)20 8400 6160   cvpub@ision.co.uk
www.tracksdirectory.ision.co.uk